FROM **HELL** TO **HEAVEN**

NAY J. RAMSEY

ISBN 978-1-0980-4098-7 (paperback)
ISBN 978-1-0980-4099-4 (digital)

Christian Faith Publishing, Inc.
832 Park Avenue
Meadville, PA 16335
www.christianfaithpublishing.com

Editing services provided by Swift Edits

Printed in the United States of America

To Taylor, my husband you are my Heaven; from the day you stepped back into my life, I knew it would be forever. You show how I'm supposed to be loved on a daily basis, and I absolutely love and admire you. You hold me, comfort me, and protect me. I feel safe with you. You are my breath of fresh air, my soul mate, and my life partner. I can't say enough how blessed I am, and how thankful I am to God for you. As long as we have each other, we'll be okay.

CONTENTS

Chapter 1: Me 7

Chapter 2: Honeymoon..11

Chapter 3: My Bundle of Pain 14

Chapter 4: Hell 26

Chapter 5: Mind Control 34

Chapter 6: Depression..39

Chapter 7: The Important Role of the Father 42

Chapter 8: Know Your Worth...48

Chapter 9: Get Out 54

Chapter 10: Heaven..57

Chapter 11: My Supernatural Childbirth 61

Epilogue: What Does *Your* Heaven Look Like?.......................67

Acknowledgments..69

CHAPTER 1

Me

Many people live their lives not knowing their purpose—not knowing why they are here on earth, or why they might have been saved from a tragic incident. Only God truly knows these things. I believe He reveals the answer to that ultimate question, "What's my purpose?" when He believes the time is right.

On a chilly night in October, my family and I were on our way home from visiting my grandparents. While making a left-hand turn, our car was t-boned by a big rig that had run a red light. Though seriously injured, we all survived. I had a fractured skull and a broken thighbone. I was only three weeks old. God protected me that night and healed me 100% from that tragic accident that should have killed me. He healed my parents and siblings too.

Today, I have no physical or medical conditions as a result of the accident. I am well and whole. I am a wife, mother, daughter, and best friend. Throughout my life, I often reflect back on the accident to remind myself that there is a reason God didn't allow me to die that night. I have a purpose—and that purpose is to share the following story with you.

I was raised in a Christian household by my mother and father, alongside my three older siblings. We lived in Suisun City, a leafy suburban town about forty-five miles northeast of San Francisco. We played in the park with friends, went on trips to Southern California and saw Disneyland and Universal Studios, and took family cruises to Mexico and Jamaica. My parents served as leaders in the children's church, and we served alongside them. I never felt like my parents put church before us, though. They achieved a good balance. We attended the local public schools, where we spent afternoons in cheerleading or football practice. I had a happy childhood and loved my family.

My parents enforced strict but understandable guidelines. Our parents wanted to protect us from prematurely being exposed to things that might negatively influence us. We were "Nickelodeon kids," meaning we watched kids shows like *Doug* and *All That*. But we weren't able to watch certain TV shows and movies that my school friends watched but my parents felt were not appropriate for us, such as the popular sitcom *Martin*, and the movie *Friday*. I remember kids coming to school and quoting lines from that movie, but I had no idea what they were talking about. I felt a little left out, or behind the times, but it wasn't that bad. We didn't listen to secular music, such as Top 40 on the radio. And of course we weren't allowed to date until we were at least seventeen years old.

Growing up, there were always a few guys who tried to flirt with my friends and me. Some even attempted to ask me out, but I always said no, because of my parents' dating rule about waiting until I was seventeen. Because I wasn't the rebellious type, and I was scared of getting caught by my dad, I played by the rules— and I was content with that. My heart, however, had other plans. When I was sixteen, a junior in high school, I fell in love. I was so smitten, I was sure this boy was "the one."

Though we were both very young at the time, I felt older than I was. I've always had an old soul. In fact, if the opportunity had presented itself, I probably would have gotten married when I was eighteen. My parents married when they were only nineteen, and after seeing how they'd done it and how they were still happily married, I felt it was reasonable to want the same thing for myself.

At sixteen, I was not focused on guys; I wasn't as boy crazy in the way a bunch of girls at my school were. But this one guy just stuck out above the others. I usually dissed guys when they tried to talk to me, partly to send the message I wasn't interested, and partly because they made me nervous. I even ended up dissing "Mr. Right," but I'm getting ahead of myself.

But this guy, Mr. Right, was not like the other guys at school. So when he asked me to our junior prom—which my parents didn't consider a "date" in the traditional sense, so I was allowed to go—I was elated. That evening was magical. He was so sweet to me, treating me like a princess; it reminded me of how my dad took care of my mom—and how he treated me. Even before the prom, this guy and I were really good friends—we'd known each other since middle school—and I wanted to keep it that way. So, though I had intense feelings for him, I resisted his efforts to make our relationship more than a friendship. This was a decision I would come to regret when I later realized just how perfect he was, at least in my eyes.

In my senior year in high school and my first couple years of college, I began to talk to more guys and explore what I liked in a man, and what I didn't like. Unfortunately, it seemed all of these young men wanted only one thing: my virginity. Trying to get to know guys while having this obstacle between us made it difficult for me to take them seriously. I mean, it was hard to have fun when it was obvious they were focused only on sex. I noticed that a lot of the guys grew bored with me when they realized I wasn't the type of girl who was willing to have sex in order to keep them around. I just wasn't. In fact, the more they wanted it, the more I realized they weren't going to get it.

Eventually, it seemed as though every guy I knew stopped talking to me because of this. After some time alone—and we're talking many long, lonely months—I decided I was ready to lose my virginity. I would take my time, but I was ready. However, not too long after doing so, I walked right into a Hell I never saw coming.

*****

My name is Nay. I'm twenty-nine years old, married to the love of my life—the one I thought was "Mr. Right," who took me to the prom, who I've been friends with since middle school. Today, we are blessed with the presence of our two sons. As I write this, I find myself reflecting back on that day so long ago when I almost died before I even had the chance to truly live. God preserved me, protected me, and healed me from that incident. But I wasn't done with challenges yet, as my life story shows. I had to go through a second Hell, one that seemed far worse to me, because I was old enough to understand every moment of it and to feel the agonizing pain of the events surrounding it.

Yet once again, God was there to catch me. His wisdom guided me and His love comforted me. I am here to tell my story and to bear witness to the power of a loving God, even after I came so close to losing all hope.

You're holding in your hands the story of how I had to go through Hell to get to Heaven. I share this because I want to help others hold on and trust. The Hell part doesn't last forever, and the Heaven on the other side is worth the fight.

CHAPTER 2

Honeymoon

It started with a poke. I noticed a young man named Eric had poked me on Facebook, so naturally, I checked his page. At the time, I was nineteen, attending college, and living with my parents. I never wanted to be with someone who had kids, but I noticed that he had a beautiful daughter and I decided I'd see what he was like anyway. I poked him back, and we started commenting on one another's pictures. Eventually, we exchanged phone numbers. Right away, he seemed very open with me, which wasn't something that I was used to. After a couple weeks, I decide to pay him a visit. At the time, I wouldn't have considered myself an alcoholic, but I did like to drink. The promise of a night out was something that appealed to me, and free drinks was definitely a way to get me to agree to a face-to-face near where he lived in the Bay Area.

When I arrived, I was caught off guard because I didn't know anything about his neighborhood—not that it mattered, since I thought of myself as just being there for the alcohol. He was from the hood, and I was from the suburbs. I didn't care where he came from, and didn't judge him for having it rough. Yet we were from two completely different worlds, trying to understand each other. After that night, we hung out a lot together; he even came to my college with me a couple times just because we wanted to be around one another.

By then, I knew exactly what I wanted in a man, and I had in my mind an ideal of the perfect relationship between a man and woman. But instead of sticking to my ideal, I chose to give the wrong man a chance. I explained to him I'd never had sex, and he responded that he couldn't believe that someone my age could still be a virgin. He never pushed or forced me to make the decision to have sex; I made it on my own. And so at nineteen, after about nine months of dating this guy, I decided I was ready to lose my virginity.

Eric knew what to say to make me believe in him. He had a car, but not a steady income. I really didn't care; he made me laugh and that was good enough. We were always together, and soon Eric became my best friend. After a while, he grew impatient with me because it took some time for me to open up and do things in bed that a more experienced girl would do. For some reason, Eric decided to stop talking to me and instead turned his attention to another girl.

Of course I felt hurt, so I also turned my attention to someone else, in an attempt to make him jealous. The truth was, I thought his dismissal of me just didn't make sense. What had I done wrong? I thought we'd been doing so well. I didn't trust his new girlfriend, and I told him she was going to play him in the end. When she did just that, he came crawling back to me. I shouldn't have taken him back after what he'd done. I should have realized a man who would leave a woman over nothing important was, well, unlikely to be a faithful companion—certainly not the kind of faithful companion I held in my mind as the ideal relationship. But again my heart won out over my head—passion over reason—and I went back to him, hoping we could work things out.

Before he left me for that trial run with the other girl, and around the time we first had sex, I told my father I was seeing a guy named Eric. My brother, a gospel rapper, had just finished his mix tape and was having a release party, so I thought it would be the perfect opportunity to have everyone in the family meet him for the first time. Usually, it can be a little nerve-wracking to meet your girlfriend's father, but Eric said he wasn't nervous at all. I wasn't in on their conversation, but Eric later said it had gone well. I was glad to hear that, because I'd had faith in what we shared together. I trusted him. And I wanted him to like my father, and vice versa.

My cousin's girlfriend at the time was able to get me a position at the place where she worked. Because it wasn't near my home but was closer to Eric's place, I thought that I could just stay with him on the days I went to work. As time progressed, I pretty much moved in with him. I was there all the time and never wanted to leave his side. I wasn't the type to need space or get tired of someone; if I love you, I love your company. At my age—I was twenty—most people pretty much knew how to date, but he was my first boyfriend and I was just getting the hang of things. We were very comfortable with each other, and if anybody tried to tell me something negative about him, I didn't listen. I was always hopeful, and I believed deep down that we would last forever.

Eric was so happy with me; he seemed proud to have me as his girlfriend. I was equally drawn to him. I didn't care about anyone else, including the other guys who tried to get with me. Sure, I felt flattered that guys were still interested in me; but my heart belonged to Eric.

Our first year together was perfect. We took trips to the beach, went to the movies, and we were always going shopping. I didn't want to be with someone who smoked—weed or cigarettes—and Eric assured me that he didn't. However, the more comfortable he got around me, the more things seemed to change. I started to smell weed around the time he started smoking Black & Mild cigars. I didn't understand how someone could hide something like that for so long—how could I have missed it?—especially knowing that I'd said from the beginning that I didn't like smokers. But I was already in so deep that I had to deal with it, so I did.

And that wasn't the only challenge I would face.

CHAPTER 3

My Bundle of Pain

Our honeymoon phase seemed to end quickly. One morning as I woke up in our apartment, I realized I had a funny feeling in my stomach. As I dressed for work, I thought more about it and realized this wasn't the first morning I'd felt this weird sensation. Almost instantly I suspected what was going on with my body—and my intuition confirmed it. I was probably pregnant.

For about a month, I was a bundle of nerves, worried about what other people—especially my family—might think if they knew I was pregnant. Of course, I wasn't yet positive; but my intuition told me I was in for a big change. Eric knew how I felt and he made jokes about it, but he didn't say anything more than that. On Mother's Day, I was sure, in a paranoid kind of way, that everyone around me would say, "Happy Mother's Day." That moment was confirmation for me; I knew, without a shadow of a doubt, that I was going to become a mother.

A few days later, I started telling my big sister Nique about the feeling I was having, and she encouraged me to take a pregnancy test. Obediently, I went to the store and picked one up. As I waited for the results, I couldn't shake the conviction I felt in the back of my mind: I knew I was pregnant. Sure enough, the test came back positive. I didn't know what to do.

I was scared, but I was used to acting tough. As a Christian, I don't believe in abortions, but that was the very first thing that came into my head. Take care of it now, so I could continue to live my life the way I had been living. I thought about my future with

Eric and about being a mother without being married first—an "unwed mother," as they call it. So I started calling around to clinics to ask about prices, to check if it was true that abortions were expensive. Turns out they were expensive—to the tune of $300, which was far more money than I had to spend. Of course, I didn't think about how much it would cost to have a baby and take care of it; this was early days.

I didn't want to face my parents with this news. One day I felt so desperate about it that I told Eric, as I used my hand to hit hard against my stomach, that I'd rather have a miscarriage than an abortion. I remember hitting my stomach over and over as if that would solve my problem.

I was so scared and upset that I didn't know what to do.

Between my own worries and my sister's advice, I decided to set up a doctor's appointment to make sure I was pregnant. I even asked that doctor how their abortion process worked. But once they hooked me up to the ultrasound machine and I saw my little peanut in there, I instantly fell in love with my baby. I began to believe that this was my seed. I had a life inside of me, and I was going to be someone's mother on January 5, 2012. I was just six weeks pregnant at the time, however, so there was still plenty of time to decide whether or not I wanted to go through with the pregnancy.

Meanwhile, the conversations I had with Eric swung back and forth between abortion and keeping the baby. "How are you going to take care of it?" he asked. "Who's going to do that if you're at work?"

"I don't know," was all I could say. "I don't know. But I think we can make this work."

Sometimes he'd smile and hold me, but other times he'd shake his head and walk out the door.

How would I raise a baby, and how would I work and pay for daycare? Wait—why was I thinking about daycare? This is my baby! I'm not going to hand him or her over to some stranger. I'm going to be the baby's mother, just like my mother was there for all of us.

15

On the other hand, Eric still didn't have a steady job, and the money he earned barely covered our rent. If I had to quit my job to stay home with my baby, would we be able to manage?

I want to tell you that I considered all of these things, but the truth is I don't remember how much I actually thought things through. In the end, I went with my gut.

A week after seeing the doctor, I took my mother out for Mother's Day lunch. It was the moment of truth. I handed her my ultrasound picture, and she asked, "What is this?"

"It's my baby," I said grinning.

She looked surprised, but I have a feeling my sister had already told her about it. "You have our support," she said. "One hundred percent." She reached her hand across the table and squeezed mine. "I can see you're worried, but you don't need to be."

I was surprised by her response, as I worried she might launch into a lecture—stuff like: *Why did you let this happen? What were you thinking? This will ruin the plans you've had!* Basically, the same stuff I had been telling myself.

Instead, it felt like a weight had been lifted off my shoulders. In that noisy restaurant, surrounded by carefree people laughing and enjoying themselves, I felt a lump in my throat and started to cry. In that moment, I felt closer to my mother than I ever had, as though we shared the same secret of motherhood. I had grown up now and was no longer her little girl.

Later that night, I handed my ultrasound picture to my dad. At the time, I was also having some ovary issues—which he knew about. So his first response was, "So, what did the doctor say the problem was?"

I burst into tears as I told him it wasn't my ovaries, but it was a picture of my baby. Once again, I dreaded the response I knew I deserved. I felt awful about how much I must have let him down—after all those years of keeping his children safe from outside temptations and crass secularism. His response surprised me as much as my mom's had. "I don't think any less of you," he said. "I will always be here to support you."

Telling my brother was a little hard, too, because I valued his opinion so much. But, like everyone else, he supported me the way that family should. I felt so relieved, but I wasn't done yet. It was time to head back out to Eric's house and explain the decision I'd made.

Eric did not react the way my family had. He wasn't too thrilled about the thought of this baby. No matter how much I tried to explain how happy I was seeing my—our—baby during the ultrasound, he remain unswayed.

"No!" he snapped. "No, you said you didn't want this baby. I'm not ready for another baby right now. I'll give you the three hundred dollars for an abortion."

My heart hit the floor. Even though a part of me knew he would react that way, I hadn't wanted to believe it. I couldn't continue the conversation, as I was getting ready for work—and still crying my eyes out. He must have seen how serious I was about keeping our baby and, as I was about to take off in my car, he yelled out the window and asked me to come back up so that we could talk more. I insisted that he come down to the car instead. He got into the passenger seat and apologized. "I'll support you," he said. He looked away, but I had seen the sincerity in his eyes. I believed him when he said he'd stay by my side throughout my pregnancy.

I didn't dare think much further ahead than nine more months of pregnancy. I didn't think about how we'd make it as parents, how we'd manage, how this little peanut would forever alter our lives. Those were thoughts for another day.

Waking up and going to sleep with my mind on my unborn child was the best feeling I've ever experienced. I would rub my belly and talk to my baby every day, every chance I got. I wanted to share those moments with Eric, but it seemed he wasn't interested. He always gave me the cold shoulder. Every week, I would check the progress of the growth of my baby. Full of excitement, I began to share pictures from a baby app that showed images of the growth of a fetus, only to deflate when Eric replied, "I know what it looks like. I have a baby already."

Of course that felt like a slap in the face. Even though he already had a daughter, I thought he'd be excited about this new little baby—the being we shared. It wasn't easy trying to get him involved and happy about our future. Luckily, my family supported me and made me feel like I could say and do anything around them. I didn't feel like I had to tiptoe around them, or pretend I wasn't excited about it. I remembered back to the time I told Eric—and myself—that I would rather have a miscarriage. How could I ever have believed such a thing?

I wasn't too far into my shift at work when I noticed that an ongoing headache I'd been having had turned into a full-blown migraine for the second day in a row. It was so bad that I couldn't even bend down or reach for something without it hurting worse. I couldn't stay at work any longer, so I decided to head back to Eric's place and let him know what was going on.

In addition to the migraine, I had also been experiencing some cramping. But I didn't think much of it, as the doctors told me it was normal for very light cramps and spotting from time to time. I called my sister, Mela, and let her know what was going on. She suggested that I make a doctor's appointment to check on the baby and myself. Next, I called my dad to fill him in on everything, and he decided to meet up with me since he was already coming home early from work.

The pain level of my cramps on a scale of one to ten—ten being excruciating—was at ten. When I walked into the hospital room, however, I felt overcome by a feeling of peace. My level of pain when down to a four; the doctor checked me and said that I was fine. Then it was time to check on my baby. The baby was swimming around, having fun, it seemed. I was so happy to see my baby actually look like a baby developing. The doctor let me hear the heartbeat, and I was filled with so much joy that I didn't want to leave. I could have stayed there forever listening to the sound of new life. The doctor took a sonogram picture at the perfect time, when the baby had its hand up as if it were waving "hi."

Little did I know it wasn't saying hello, but waving goodbye.

My dad met me back home so I could rest and take it easy for a while. As I lay down, the pain came back and hit me like a ton of bricks. Between the on-and-off cramping and my continued migraine, I ended up holding an ice pack to my forehead in an attempt to ease all the pain I was in. When that didn't help, I went outside. My dad was washing his car, and I sat on a chair nearby and explained how much agony I was experiencing. I was taking deep breaths and rubbing my stomach. It felt like I needed to make a bowel movement.

"Hey," my dad joked, scrubbing the tires, "if it helps, do what you have to do."

So I went in, took care of business, went back outside, and sat down. When he asked if I felt better, I told him no, and that I thought I needed to go again.

As I was sitting on the toilet, I began to cry and pray. "God, please don't let me lose my baby," I whispered, because somehow I knew I was about to lose my baby. Just the way I'd known that I was pregnant in the first place. In my moment of crying out, I felt what I thought was the baby coming out. (I found out later it was only tissue.) I immediately started screaming.

It was all over in a split second—no pain, no thoughts, and no noise.

Then I heard my sister's voice as she banged on the bathroom door; it sounded like muffled, as though we were underwater. Then I snapped back to myself and bent over. I could barely walk, but I shuffled over and opened the door.

Holding her own baby in her arms, Nique tried to help me stay standing, and called out for my dad. My dad didn't understand what was going on; all he knew was that I was in pain and yelling about my baby being in the toilet. He moved as quickly as possible. Blood was gushing out of me like a waterfall, so my sister wrapped a towel around my waist, and my dad hustled me to his car and drove me to the hospital. As he was driving, I could still feel blood coming out. By then I was a little delusional, moaning and crying the entire time.

When we got to the hospital, my dad grabbed a wheel-chair while the receptionist asked a bunch of questions. My dad explained things, giving as many details as he could and saying that I had just made twelve weeks that day. Meanwhile, I was beginning to accept the fact that I was losing the thing—the baby, the person—who was the most important thing in my life. That was when I felt my baby move its way slowly down from my uterus, preparing to leave my body.

"It's all right," I told my dad, though I was partly delusional and definitely trying to make myself believe it. "This is meant to be. It's what God wants. I don't need a baby at this moment in my life, and God is allowing this to happen for a reason." I spoke quietly so no one else in the ER could hear.

"No, it'll be all right," he said, leaning down to take my hand and squeeze it. "You'll be fine." When the nurses came and told me to stand up, I felt the baby come rolling out. It was inside my underwear. When I told the nurses that my baby was in my pants, they didn't do anything. They were just trying to help me the best way that they knew how. One of the nurses started to examine me, and all I could remember him saying was, "Yea, there's no baby." He must have said that at least ten times.

I was still in a lot of pain and didn't want anyone touching me. My dad stayed by my side, keeping me calm. Finally the pain medicine started kicking in. My dad helped me dial my cell phone to call Eric.

Through woozy tears—unyielding grief mixed with disorient-ing pain meds—I said, "It's gone. We lost our baby."

I couldn't tell by his reaction whether he was happy or sad for us. I probably shouldn't have been thinking about his reaction, worrying about his reaction. It should have been enough that I was devastated, right? I was lucky to have my father there with me. But I wanted Eric to be there, too—not because I wanted him to cheer me up, because that wasn't going to happen. But because I had been thinking of our new little family. Now that our family was down to two, I wanted to be with the other member—the father, my partner, my love.

"I'll find a way to get there," he said. "Might take a while." He didn't have a car at the time, so he would ask to use his mother's. As I waited for him in that sterile hospital room, my brother and three sisters came to see me.

While we were all talking, I could feel my stomach contracting. The doctor said it was part of the process of shedding the tissue from my uterus. I was told that I had an infection, was running a fever, and that the tissue wasn't shedding as fast as it should. That meant I had to have an emergency D&C surgery. The one person I really wanted was my mom, but unfortunately she was in Texas visiting my grandma. We talked on the phone and she insisted on coming, but I told her to stay with Grandma and enjoy her trip. I called Eric to tell him I'd be heading into surgery, and he said he was still trying to convince his mom to let him use her truck. I explained to him how much I needed him. Even though I had my family's support, I still wanted him there. I thought about how selfish his mom was being. As a woman, how could she be so callous? My brother, his wife, and my dad kissed me goodbye as I headed off to surgery—which lasted only about twenty minutes.

Next thing I knew, I awoke to find myself in a different room in front of my dad and my sister Nique. I was admitted into a room for recovery and to monitor my fever. There was still no sign of Eric. The long night transitioned into morning, and every time I went to the bathroom, I started crying. I would cry from the pain in my gut, only to start screaming because it reminded me of the tissue coming out when I first discovered that I was losing my baby.

Coincidentally, my friend Christine hit me up on Facebook that night to ask me how I was. I didn't want anyone visiting me, but I had to tell her the truth. With no hesitation, she dropped what she was doing to come and visit me. Christine and I have been friends for years, and she's always been there for me. I decided to call Eric one more time. When he answered, I went off. I felt that his mom just didn't want him to be there and that he wasn't trying hard enough to make that happen. He could've asked my sisters or my dad to pick him up. He could have even taken the bus. If he really wanted to be there for me, he would have made some kind of effort.

By the third day, I knew Eric wasn't coming, and later that evening I was released from the hospital fever free.

My dad and I decided that we wanted some pizza, so we stopped off at our favorite local pizza place. There, I got a phone call from Eric saying his mom was going to let him use the truck, but that he had to bring his older brother. How ironic; the day I come home from the hospital he was finally allowed to use the truck? So I let him know when I got home so that he could come by. I went to my room and tried to lie down until he came, but immediately burst into tears and realized that I just couldn't be alone. My dad told me to go lie in my parents' bed. When Eric showed up, I didn't really know what to say or how to feel. I didn't want his brother seeing me, because I was a mess and because his brother may have been happy that the baby was no longer in our lives. He'd told Eric that once our new baby was in the picture that Eric would probably forget his daughter. In fact, I didn't want to see or be seen by anyone at that moment.

We all sat down, and Eric handed me a card from his mother; all I could say was thank you. I wanted to explain what had happened, but I couldn't talk about something so personal with his brother there. Eric said he wanted to go to the park to play basketball, and he wanted me to come with him and his brother, clearly oblivious to the fact that I had just gotten out the hospital after being bedridden for three days. It didn't seem to occur to him that I wouldn't have the strength or energy to go to the park. But I wanted to be with him, so I thought I would give it a try and just sit on a bench.

So we went, and I walked slowly and deliberately, as I felt unsteady on my feet. Eric and his brother shot hoops while I watched. Eric must have sensed how annoyed I was because he stopped for a minute and tried to talk to me. However, between the setting and the presence of his brother, I just didn't feel like having a conversation, so I asked if he could take me back home because I felt weak and tired. When we got there, his brother stayed in the car while Eric and I finally had a moment alone in my living room. He began to say that he was sorry that I had to go through what I had and that he hadn't been there with me. I explained how the events went down, with a few details I could remember, but it was getting late and I knew he needed to head back home. I told him I would return to our apartment when I felt up to it.

As the days went by, I cried every day about everything. One night, we were lying down and I started talking about losing the baby only to burst into tears. I was so emotional during this period. I'd never felt that kind of pain before, and Eric didn't know how to deal with a grieving girlfriend. One day, I tried to explain to him how devastating the whole experience was for me. Instead of lifting me up, however, he put me down. He said things like, "It's been months now, you should be over it" and "My mom's been through way more miscarriages. She's stronger than you" and "You're weak, woman up, and stop using this miscarriage as ammunition to make people feel bad." I yelled back that our baby had been my seed, a part of me that I couldn't get back, and that it made sense that I felt empty. My outburst left him speechless.

There were sleepless nights where I found myself thinking about what it would have been like to carry my baby full term, and I couldn't stop the tears from flowing. I cried for the lost baby, and I cried for the lost opportunity to be a mother. There were days when I would just walk into my parents' room with my arms out for my mom to catch me in her lap while I cried. I felt like no one understood me because they had not experienced what I'd gone through.

Finally, about six months after my miscarriage, Eric became more supportive and started to hold me more. I felt like he was listening to me, and that he was taking me seriously. One night, on our way back to his place from my house, we began to argue. I felt he hadn't wanted our child, and his mother and oldest brother didn't seem to care too much either. So as loud and disrespectful as he was, he called his mom and brother so that all of us could sit down and I could let them know how I felt.

On the night in question, I was so broken that my voice trembled as I spoke. I started with his mother and explained to her, stuttering and breathing heavily, what it had been like for me to experience such a traumatic situation. She should have dropped everything and brought him to me, I said, because I thought she cared for me. We'd always gotten along, and from her own experiences, she should've understood how I felt and the importance of him being there with me.

"Well, sweetie," she responded, "I didn't want to take the chance with my truck breaking down, and he got to you when he could."

In my mind, that just showed me how selfish she was. I didn't believe that was why she didn't let Eric take her truck. Instead, she probably didn't want him seeing me like that, or she simply hadn't given the situation enough thought. By that point I was crying, partially out of anger and partially because I was hurt. When I confronted his brother about not being supportive of my pregnancy, he said, "No, it wasn't that. I just didn't want my brother being distracted and forgetting that he has a daughter already."

I said, "Well, that's his job as a man—to be responsible and provide for both children. Besides, I'm the one always telling him to get his baby girl."

I felt like I wasn't getting any support from Eric at all; he was yelling, telling them that all I did was complain and get on his case for not being there. All of which was very true. It was the main reason why I had called my baby "mine" and not "ours."

I'd never felt so alone, hurt, and empty. I knew to pray, but I didn't know exactly what was going on with me. Every day, I would relive the pain of my baby coming out of me in that wheelchair. I couldn't use my downstairs bathroom for months because of the memory of it, and when I had my monthly cycle, I cried because the pain reminded me of that tragic day. It felt like my days just wouldn't get brighter. I began to realize that I was at the lowest point I'd ever been in life and I couldn't see the light for anything. I was taught to have faith and know that God was always present, and would heal me and bless me; and I knew that the Lord would gift me with another child when I got married someday. But I just didn't want to go through all of it again. Not anytime soon, anyway.

*****

If there was a glimmer of hope for me, it was in the sign I received from God just before I lost the baby. I remember when I was pregnant waking up one morning smiling because God had shown me something I took to be a promise of peace to come. About a week before my miscarriage, I dreamed I was in the delivery room giving birth. My dad was in the corner of the room (he was the only one there), yelling, "The baby is coming out. Get the doctor!"

The baby slid right out, and at the end of my dream all I could remember was the doctor holding my baby near my face, and I could see it was a girl. I told my mom about this because she also has a gift of dreaming, and she said it didn't sound all that positive. But I wanted to be hopeful, so I took it to mean that I would have a smooth delivery. Obviously, that hadn't been the case. There was a reason why my dad had been the only one there in my dream, because he would turn out to be the only one there when it happened. God had left me with the knowledge that it had been a baby girl, and that offered a small measure of closure.

CHAPTER 4

Hell

After dating Eric for a while, I started to grow numb to the noisy, chaotic neighborhood where we lived. It was a small studio in an apartment building, and sometimes at night I heard gunshots and sirens—nothing like the suburban home I grew up in. Even so, I never felt truly safe in my new environment. My dad and I were still close, even though he didn't agree with my relationship. He would always ask me if I was okay and if I felt safe; I would tell him that I was fine. However, hearing gunshots every couple of days, and worrying that Eric would get shot on his way back home from the corner store eventually took its toll. I started to have dreams of death, specifically of men breaking down the door and trying to rob us. I had these dreams all the time, but I never spoke to anyone about them. Instead, I chose to pray.

Walking outside at night and even going to the grocery store, I always looked over my shoulder. I never felt safe and secure, including when I was with Eric. Getting first his rims and then his car stolen only made me think about what could happen to my own car. After a while, it wore me out. I got tired of being there. It would get to the point where I was going to motels and staying in other areas because I just wanted to get away from his place. The way I was raised, I knew better than to stay in a dirty, unsafe motel, yet that's exactly what I did plenty of times.

Usually Eric would stay with me, but it seemed like every time we went to a motel, something went wrong. One time, we got into an argument, and he decided to leave knowing that his phone was off and there would be no way for me to contact him. Another time we decided to get away, and he had a very difficult night crying about an incident that he had not forgiven himself for. He sat on the bed, I stood in front of him, and he held me tight. His grip started to hurt and I warned him that he didn't want to hit me and that he shouldn't allow his anger to take over the situation. This went on for at least two hours, and I finally got him to relax enough to eventually fall asleep.

A couple of hours later, he woke up out of his sleep and started throwing up. I hopped out of the bed, grabbed the trash can, and gave it to him. At that point, I was just through with everything and tired of trying to always be superwoman. On top of that, I didn't do well with people throwing up, so I left him there.

As I said before, Eric and I liked to drink a lot during this time. It's what brought us together in the first place. There were times when I didn't drink as much as he did, however, and I just wanted him to stop. Whenever Eric drank too much, things seemed to get worse between us. For instance, I can't stand being pinched. It hurts, and I can't take the pain. Eric knew this but did it anyway. He would also embarrass me when we were out with friends; he was rude to our waiters or anyone with authority if things were too slow or not going his way. One time, we were out eating with some friends of ours while he was still drunk and he started pinching my leg underneath the table. I smiled it off while telling him under my breath to stop—hoping that nobody was looking—but he kept doing it. As a joke, he wanted me to think. He knew how much it hurt me, yet he continued to do it until I got up. I wanted to avoid causing a scene. Yet I couldn't help but feel upset—and confused. Here he was, pinching me purposely to get me upset, knowing that it hurt me, and this was supposed to be love?

The tension between the two of us was obvious, and I noticed myself being distant at times because I didn't want to deal with him or his mess. Did I love him, or was I just with him because I didn't want to be alone? Was this the way all relationships felt—some days good, some days bad? I felt so conflicted.

And then there were the issues around intimacy. I'll admit that there were times when I didn't know the difference between just having sex and making love. I always wanted to believe that we were making love because I loved him, but that's the opposite of what was going on. It wasn't easy at times, trying to please him, because he was my first and I didn't know exactly what to do all the time. We'd been together for about a year and a half, and our sex life wasn't as pleasing to me anymore. There were multiple times when I would tell him to please stop because he was hurting me; though whether he was sober or not, he still would do whatever he wanted. My tears and the pain in my voice didn't seem to bother him or catch his attention. He kept right on with what he was doing, and didn't stop until he was finished.

"Why are you crying?" he'd ask, frustrated. "You're weak because you can't take it like a real woman would."

I'd say things like, "Belittling me as your girlfriend just makes things worse. I can't help the fact that you're hurting me, and you should stop when I tell you to stop."

As many times as this occurred, I didn't realize that his actions were actually rape. Though I loved him and he claimed that he loved me, when I said "stop," it meant stop. But I was young and didn't realize I had the right to insist he treat me better, so I continued to stay with him. I knew how to forget really fast so that we could move on from the situation, but one night I wasn't in the mood to have sex. I lay down, and Eric started to kiss me. He was a little more forceful than usual. I told him I wasn't in the mood, but he didn't care; he kept going. When I started to push him off, he pinned me down and pulled down my pants. I was crying and repeatedly telling him to get off of me, to please stop and not to do this.

My cries went ignored.

"Lord, please don't let this happen to me," I begged silently. "Don't let him do this to me."

It wasn't until I started kicking, hitting, and scratching that he finally got up. It amazes me how, when I reach out to God, he always comes through during times of trouble.

"Why would you do that?" I asked. "What were you thinking?"

"I don't know," he said, "I blacked out. That wasn't me. I'm sorry."

In that moment I was terrified, confused, and in disbelief. I was in so much shock, and I kept thinking, *"Why is this happening to me, what did I do to deserve this, why am I still with him?"*

I had no good answer to any of those questions.

*****

I loved Eric, but he controlled me, and I didn't even realize that it was happening. It wasn't so much verbal control—him always telling me what to do. Instead, it was emotional control. After I lost my baby, I lost myself and just wasn't the girl he'd first met. Eric didn't know how to build me up because he was too busy watching me fall. Which is exactly what I continued to do. I hid my unhappiness, but everyone who really knew me could see it beneath the mask. He was a constant source of stress and reinforced my feeling of loss. I was so lost that I didn't know who else to turn to except for him. I even bought a puppy to help me cope, but I was so unhappy I had to give him away after only five months.

His daughter's second birthday was approaching, and since I worked at a toy store, I could get good gifts at a discount. I loved showering her with gifts, because I loved her just as much as I loved her father. I wasn't able to be at her birthday party, but I did show up later after work. I didn't have the typical baby mama drama—by which I mean trouble getting along with the baby's mama—like most people, so seeing and being around her wasn't a problem. Tiffany, the mother of Eric's daughter, shared a birthday with her, so once I arrived the celebration had become more of an adult thing. Alcohol and weed were going around, and I wasn't too happy about that because by then watching Eric and the others get drunk and high all of the time was getting irritating. Everything seemed normal at first, but I was honestly ready to go after only twenty minutes of being there. After an hour and a half, we decided to leave to grab something to eat. Our car ride back home was a little weird, and I couldn't figure out why he was so angry. He didn't want to touch me when we finally got home, so I left him alone.

A few weeks passed before I got a message from Tiffany on Facebook that was devastating. She explained that she and Eric had had sex at the party and she knew that he wasn't going to tell me, so she felt the need to say something. She went on and on about how sorry she was, and my heart sank into my stomach. He was across the room putting on his daughter's pajamas when I set the laptop down and walked to the bathroom. I immediately called my sister Mela, crying, and asking for advice because I had never been through something like this before. She told me to wipe my tears, take a deep breath, and simply ask him about it, since I needed to find out the truth. In my heart, I knew he had done it, but I went back into the room and asked him anyway.

"Did you sleep with her mother? You don't have to lie, just tell me the truth."

While he was still preparing his daughter for bed, he looked down and said "no." I asked him one more time, and he still said the same thing. So I got up and started to grab my things. That's when all hell broke loose. When Eric realized that I was calling it quits, he came after me.

"What are you doing?" he demanded, "Nah, you're not about to do this."

He started to back me up against the dresser. I felt threatened and just needed him to get off me, so I started pushing at him. When he wouldn't stop, I started swinging. After hitting him multiple times I must have blacked out, because I just lost it and kept hitting him. I felt the blow to my eye, but I never saw his hand. Eric hugged me tight against him because he knew what he'd done. I started screaming and yelling, telling him to let me go. Frightened, the baby started yelling and crying.

Eric's mother and brother came into the apartment from their place next door to break us up and grab the baby. Eric threw my purse out of the two-story building, and his mom went out to get it for me. I was shouting at him to let me go and he finally did.

My eye was watering and I could barely see out of it. Meanwhile Eric was bellowing and hitting the walls. His mother defended Eric, saying she knew for certain he hadn't done anything with Tiffany because she'd been there the whole time and the two were never off together alone. It was impossible. She also said that all Tiffany wanted to do was break up Eric's and my happy home.

But I didn't believe her. I knew Eric, and he wouldn't have reacted that way—so defensively, so violently—if he'd been innocent. I wanted nothing more than to escape, so I walked outside. Eric was still going on about how he hadn't done anything, hoping to convince me to come back. But I was numb.

"How low can you go to hit me?" I asked, and he instantly denied the accusation. He said that I must have run into his elbow while he was trying to block my hits. I thought it was a bunch of bull, but I listened anyway. My response surprised me; Eric apologized, and I said, "I already forgave you for cheating and for putting your hands on me."

Right before I agreed to go home for the night, he told me that Tiffany had only performed oral sex on him, and that was it. At that time, that's what I believed. He asked if I could come back up instead of going home, but I couldn't stand to see his face.

I drove off.

On my way home—to my parents' place—I couldn't believe what had just gone down. Now I would have to face my family with a black eye. I went upstairs immediately and let Mela know what had happened. She was shocked and told me that I would have to tell our dad. I walked back downstairs and met my dad's eyes.

"He hit me," I said, then looked back down. My dad was speechless and bowed his head. I began to explain what had happened, and all the while my dad stayed calm—which wasn't normal for any father who learned his daughter had been beaten by her boyfriend. I didn't want to wake my brother, so I took a picture of my eye and sent it to him that night. He called around 7 a.m. the next morning, very upset. It was like trying to have a conversation with Bruce Banner right before he transformed into the Hulk. I heard him screaming and crying for me over the phone; who wouldn't react the same way for their baby sister? I had to give my phone to my dad to try and calm him down. All I could think about was how my actions had hurt the people closest to me.

Later that evening, my brother and I were on the phone all night long, trying to figure out how Eric could have done this to me. I was the person that had been there since day one and supported him when I didn't have to. The fact that I had to wake up the next day and go to work didn't make it any better, because the bruising around my eye was noticeable. But my focus was on earning an income, and I'd just gotten a promotion, so I didn't want to miss out on anything. I tried hard to hide it, but the black eye was obvious—and embarrassing.

In fact, I'd never been so embarrassed. Here I was, a victim of domestic violence. My boss, Tim, was like an uncle to some of us, and when I walked into the office, the first thing he said to me was, "Did he hit you?"

Mind you, I've never talked to Tim about my relationship, but being a father himself he seemed to understand what had happened to me. I laughed, "No," I told him. "I'm fine, don't worry about it."

"Don't ever go back to him," he said, clearly unconvinced. "Any man who puts his hands on you doesn't deserve you, and he's a punk for that."

At that moment, all I could do was agree and say "thank you."

I told myself I wouldn't see him again until I was ready. I'm not sure why I would even want to, but I was already in too deep. Eric couldn't believe how serious I was, but that same night, I changed my relationship status on Facebook. But that wasn't enough to make me stay away. After three weeks, I decided to go talk to him. That was the longest we'd ever been apart. At first, I could barely look at him, and it was very awkward. We talked for a while and ended up having make-up sex. I know how dumb I was to go back and do the very thing that had started the fight. In fact, that was the worst decision I could have ever made; now he really had me in his complete control.

I was still working near where he lived, which only made it easier to stop off a few times to see him before or after work. Seeing his mother and brother was embarrassing because I felt stupid going back to him after they had witnessed the whole fight. Everyone acted like things were back to normal, and of course I did too. Yet I never forgot what Eric had done to me—and with his former girlfriend. I just was really good at forgetting—or perhaps pretending to myself that I could forget it—and ignoring everything he had done, while keeping my hurt to myself.

But let's rewind. There had been signs before all this happened—signs that I had ignored. When we first got together, I asked him if he had ever put his hands on a woman and he'd told me yes. He said he was used to women hitting him and causing fights. He told me that he'd beaten his ex up really badly and then laughed about how bad he'd messed up her face.

I told myself, "Oh, he won't put his hands on me." But there had been several incidents leading up to the big punch that should've made me want to leave. Instead, I chose to stay. I remembered talking to him, sitting on top of him, and joking around. Laughing, I'd hit him in his face. I guess he didn't find it very funny because he slapped me back, pushed me off of him, and told me not to do it again. He moved over to the couch while I started crying in disbelief.

"Why did you hit me?" I yelled. I couldn't believe it. "No— not me—why?"

Red flag number two: Since he loved arguing, our disagreements always turned into a brawl. Once, he grabbed my jacket as I was trying to pull away it and ripped. The third red flag was that while on the phone with a friend, he got upset with me and we ended up on the floor where he then ripped my shirt all the way off. I laughed it off at the time, surprised that he was so upset. Though I found out what was wrong eventually (allowing that kind of behavior in our relationship gave him more room for further abuse), that didn't negate the signs that were there. However, instead of listening to the warning bells going off in my head, I ignored the warnings and hoped for the best.

CHAPTER 5

Mind Control

I was very private about going back to Eric after he'd cheated on and hit me. Knowing that I was back with him could only hurt my family even more, so I lied to them. I knew I shouldn't be with him, and that our relationship was not good for either of us, but I was comfortable enough with him because it felt so familiar. After all, I'd been with this man for three years. We always talked about our future and how we just wanted to get away from everyone because I knew no one would be happy about us, and so did he. It seemed like I was frustrated all the time instead of being happy. Plus, I was still having trouble trying to get over my miscarriage.

Yet I stuck by him. Even when I wasn't with him, my heart was. Every time another man hit on me or asked me out, I would decline because I wanted to remain loyal to Eric, even though he didn't expect me to. Meanwhile, he was still in the same headspace and had no job, no money, and was just barely getting by. It was hard not to feel sorry for him. He didn't have the support of a family like I did, and I felt like *I* was his family. If I didn't support him, nobody else was going to. So I continued to buy him groceries, clothes, and even shoes when I thought he needed them.

I usually celebrated Christmas on Christmas Eve and didn't really do much on Christmas morning, so one year I agreed to take Eric and his brothers over to their aunt's house because they rarely got to see their family. It was great to see them all reunite after so many years, but it was getting late for me and I had to head back home. I explained that to Eric and he got upset. "You always get to see your family," he said. "I never get to see mine. You're being selfish."

"No, I'm not," I replied. "It's getting late. I live forty-five minutes away, and I need to head back home."

I didn't want his family to see us arguing or feel the vibe we were giving off, so I decided to drop it for a minute. Then his brother said, "You're the best woman my brother has ever had, real talk. I'm happy you guys are working it out."

In the back of my mind, I'm thinking, *Really? After you witnessed me in both situations being physically and emotionally hurt? Shut up.* I was just about done after that. I told Eric I was ready to go, and he still wasn't having it. We walked outside, and he started yelling at me. He said that I didn't love him because if I did, I would stay. I explained how I wasn't going to argue with him and he continued to yell. It was 11:00 p.m. and he was making a scene. When he kicked down the neighbor's trash can, I started to get upset. I thought he was about to kick my brand-new car, so I threatened to leave.

Instead of reacting like a normal person, though, he started to walk away instead of going back into his aunt's house. I called his brother to come outside and try to stop him, but it didn't work. All I could think of was how late it was. I worried about his safety my whole way home. I called him over and over, but he didn't answer. I stayed up all night, literally worried sick. I couldn't even eat until I'd heard from him. I texted his brother to see if he had heard from Eric or if he made it back, which he finally did that evening. I couldn't believe he'd actually done something like that, knowing that I would be worried. But obviously, he didn't care. Typical Eric. I explained how dangerous his actions had been and how much doing things like that just stressed me out.

Eric apologized but there were so many times throughout our relationship where he would just leave—just walk away from me, from our problems, and from any opportunity to work things out. I despised him for doing it. I couldn't stand the feeling of looking dumb in front of other people. There were numerous occasions where we would argue and he'd slam the door and go next door to his brother's. It seemed like he got a kick out of leaving me in public. I remember my cousin invited me to her bonfire. At that time we weren't together, but I still took him places with me. We got into an argument yet again, and when we arrived at the bonfire, Eric decided to stay in the car. My cousin Jasmine asked where Eric was, and I rolled my eyes and said he was still in the car. So there I was, alone amongst friends, yet again looking dumb. I mean, what kind of girl would continue to hang out with such a temperamental guy?

I texted him over and over to get out, but he said he'd get out when he felt like it. As awkward as that had been, he finally dragged himself to the bonfire, only to try to start another argument with me. I decided to leave and as we were walking away, he strode ahead of me like I was not even there. An older couple walking past reprimanded him, saying, "Never leave your lady behind you, young man."

I just looked on with embarrassment; yet again he'd left me. Whether we were at the grocery store or the mall, Eric was forever abandoning me. Especially when I needed him the most.

Twilight is one of my favorite movies. (So much so that I own all of the films in the series) So, Eric and I decided to go see the latest installment when it came out in theaters. We went to a movie theater we've never been to before because I wanted to shop a little in a place out of the way from where I lived. As usual, Eric started an argument with me and got upset because I'd gotten lost. It was like I could never get a break from him or the constant bickering. He didn't have the money, so I paid for our tickets—something I was used to. I told him I would buy some snacks as well. When we sat down, I told him that I didn't have that much money. He started to flip out.

"But you said we were going to get food and snacks," he yelled. "A hot dog isn't enough!"

People were starting to look at us because he was getting loud, complaining about not getting enough food. I kept trying to explain how expensive the food was and how we had to get either one thing or the other, but not both. He stormed off to the concession stand and came back with a hot dog, still upset with me. On our way back to his place, we argued about the situation with the food. The more intense the argument got, the more menacing he became. There was a drink in my cup holder and he threatened to throw the contents of it on me.

"Do it," I said.

So, as I was driving on the freeway in the middle of traffic, a cup of soda was thrown in my face and landed on my lap.

"So let me guess, you gonna start crying?" he asked.

"No," I said, "I'm not. I actually don't have anything to cry about anymore. How can you say you love me if you keep hurting me? That's not love. I'd throw you out of this car right now, but I actually love you enough not to."

"Well, you shouldn't have told me to do it," he reasoned. "I'm the type that if you dare me to do something, I will."

The whole way back I was full of pain and frustration. I felt dumb. *Why are you dealing with this when you deserve better?*

It's like Eric knew exactly what he was doing; he had control of me emotionally and took over my mind. The fact that I hid him from my family gave him the advantage in a way, and certainly left me feeling more alone and without recourse. I did talk about him from time to time with my family to see what kind of reaction I got, and it was lackluster at best. They didn't like him, but they didn't feel it was within their rights to tell me to leave him.

Eric was still very harsh and rude. I remember calling him one day while I was at work and getting into an argument. He finally came out and said the one thing I'd been waiting for him to say. After being with him for three years, he finally decided to call me the "B" word. Like any other fed-up woman would have, I called him one too, told him to never call me again, and hung up. Later he eventually apologized, which I accepted, of course. I always said that I'd never stay with a man who treated me the way that Eric was treating me, but I just loved him too much to leave him. I had a lot of emotions going through my mind. My head said I should leave him alone and find someone new, but my heart said stay.

By the end of 2012, almost four years after we'd started dating, I finally decided I couldn't take any more. I wanted to get right with God and reestablish my relationship with him once and for all. I stopped listening to secular music and went back to church. Eric pretended to act like he wanted to follow me, so of course I tried to encourage him. My brother is a gospel rapper, and he had just released his mix tape not that long ago, so Eric was always listening to the music and said that it was really helpful. I thought it was a great step, but the cursing didn't stop and neither did the arguing, yelling, drinking, or smoking. But once I decided to make that change, slowly but surely I began to drift away from him.

CHAPTER 6

Depression

After the miscarriage, I noticed I always felt nauseous after a meal. To the point where I would almost throw up. I remember celebrating my sister Mela's birthday and drinking a little alcohol. I knew then that my stomach was sensitive, but I didn't know to what extent until that night. We went home and were falling asleep when I got this sensation in my stomach. It hit my whole body, and I thought that I was going to vomit. It was difficult to stand up, but I went straight to my parents' room, crying, and asked them to take me to the emergency room because the pain felt so intense.

The ER technicians did an ultrasound, and the doctor came back and said that there wasn't really anything showing besides my liver being a little larger than normal. Otherwise, it was nothing too serious. In that moment, I felt that my drinking days were over, and that was going to be a big change, because people who knew me knew that I drank alcohol all the time.

It was definitely a sign from God.

Even though Eric and I were broken up, I still kept in contact with him. He wanted to see me, but I knew that wasn't going to actually happen. I had one appointment after the other to treat the problem with my liver. It was very difficult for me, since it had to do with my stomach. I had to get so many ultrasounds done, and each one just reminded me of my baby. Even with all of this going on, I was still connected with Eric and I was still as stressed out and unhappy as when we'd been dating.

While I was going through the motions, I still wasn't able to eat as much as I had been eating. I noticed that I began to lose weight. In fact, every time I went to an appointment, I was down a few more pounds. I didn't really see it as a problem. I just thought I couldn't keep food down. When I ate pizza, a slice was enough to make me feel full. With something like a burger, I could only take two bites before my stomach rebelled. Ginger ale became my best friend. There were certain prescriptions that I was put on, but none of them worked, so I only ate once or twice a day. It was hard for me to focus at work, and it was just more stress on top of all my relationship problems. My boss was very hard to get along with as well, and everything just seemed to be piling up.

From time to time, I would miss work because I would have attacks after eating certain foods. It was tricky because I could eat a burger and be fine one day, and then the next second it would trigger my stomach and cause an attack. This would happen every few months, and I would have to miss the next day of work so that I could recover. One particular night, I woke up and my whole body was shaking and there was an aching pain in my stomach. Once again, I went to the emergency room. When the doctor came back and said that he'd found polyps in my gallbladder, I began to cry. I'd done research and I knew that polyps could be cancerous. At that point, I was just extremely tired from multiple ultrasounds, taking different medications, and undergoing MRI and CT scans. It was a lot of pressure on me and nothing was being solved. Overall, I ended up losing 25 pounds.

Being with Eric only brought unhappiness, and seeing him kept me in a rut because I couldn't stop thinking about the loss of my baby. I decided I'd see him one last time. It was the day before Valentine's Day, and I had a feeling that I wouldn't get a thing from him. I just wanted to hope for something different but there was no card, no candy, nothing. We drove past people selling teddy bears, flowers, and candy, but he didn't budge. I look over at him, and he started to cry.

"Why are you crying?" I asked.

"I'm so sorry for hurting you, I know I messed up big time. I can tell I'm losing you."

I was numb to what he was saying. The old me would've cried with him and fell for it all, but I just sat there.

"Yes, you did mess up," I told him, "and there's nothing you can do to fix it."

That was the last day I saw him.

I remember driving home from work one day and calling my brother to tell him that I was finally free from the whole situation. I no longer felt like the loss of my baby controlled me. I had two pink balloons with my ultrasound picture in the middle hanging on the wall in my room. When I decided to take them down, that's when I knew I was at peace. The moment I let my baby go was the moment I was able to let Eric go.

Peace overcame upon me, followed closely by joy. Eric called me over and over, and it was becoming easier not to pick up my phone. I started to get fearful even though I knew I shouldn't. That fact that he knew where I worked was concerning because he would joke that he was going to come up there. I immediately threatened to call the police if he ever did. Back then nobody knew that he was truly like a monster—though one that I loved. He eventually stopped trying to contact me. I prayed, trusted, and believed that God would take control over the situation, and he did.

CHAPTER 7

The Important Role of the Father

A lot of women can't say they had a father to guide and show them how a real man is supposed to treat and nurture a young lady. I am blessed to say that I had one, and still have one now. He taught me not to depend on a man and, if I wanted anything, to work for it. I always had a job and didn't want for anything. He also taught his kids how to fix things—he even taught me how to change a tire. Throughout this relationship, my dad never once neglected me or treated me like he didn't care; he knew that in order to maintain the relationship he had to be slow to speak and quick to listen. I knew I could go to my dad for just about anything, just as I knew that Eric wasn't the kind of man who would take care of me.

My dad always came through for me during my relationship with Eric. There were many times when I had car trouble and my dad got up in the middle of the night, or stopped whatever he was doing, to take that thirty-minute drive to rescue me. Eric acted like he couldn't do a thing, but I could tell it bothered him how close we were and how my dad always came through for me every single time I needed him.

I've always had a special relationship with my dad, but having him experience what I went through made our bond even stronger. He almost lost me as a baby, and then he had to watch me physically lose my baby right in front of him. It was very difficult for me to go through that, but I don't think I would have been able to maintain myself if my dad wasn't there helping me get through it. Most fathers wouldn't have been able to watch their child go through what I had, let alone stay for every moment of it. Usually, a man would think that my miscarriage was a woman's concern and want out right away. But not my dad; my dad couldn't, wouldn't, leave my side.

There are a number of lessons I've picked up over the years. If my relationship with Eric taught me anything, it was wisdom. Yes, it took me a while to learn that lesson, and there was a lot of trial and error (okay, way too many errors). But I grew in wisdom, and I'm glad for that.

The lessons that my dad imparted and what I learned about myself when I realized that I was pregnant have stayed with me. For one thing, a parent needs to be constant. They need to love unconditionally, and let their child know they're always there for them. Sometimes it's going to be easy to show that unconditional love—like when the parent is at their child's school play or high school football game. There's so much to be proud about, and to stand tall with other parents. But other times it will be hard to stand strong, like when the child is in trouble or in the hospital losing her baby. And those are the times when it's most important to be the kind of parent you'd want your child to have. That is the kind of father I was lucky enough to have.

Here are a few points I learned from my father as a role model. I share them with you in hopes that they will help other fathers—and mothers—be supportive, caring, and loving parents to their children, in the way that God is a parent to each of us.

Key Points for Being a Stellar Father to a Daughter

- Wisdom. Even before your daughter is born, you prepare. This starts by asking God for wisdom, courage, and strength.

- Nurture. Every day of your child's life, you nurture and love her. You remind her how beautiful, precious, and important she is.
- Influence. The influence you have over your daughters is the key to their success in everything they do, including relationships with their significant other.
- Creative. Parents need to be creative and think outside the box. Challenges will come up, and this demands that parents act quickly—and every child will bring different challenges and circumstances. Be creative in the way you help your children solve their problems.

My dad has three daughters in all, and God showed him how to handle all of us in different ways because we are all unique individuals. I always felt loved and beautiful because I had a dad that made sure I felt that way. He ensured that I knew that about myself so I didn't need to look for it in a man—even though I made a few mistakes and spent too long testing it to see if it was true. (It was.) In my situation, he made sure he influenced my life so he could affect my character in a positive way. Even though he didn't agree with all the decisions I made, I knew I could still go to him when I needed to because I knew that I was important. He always made himself available. My dad's influence on my life helped me walk away from my toxic relationship.

My dad taught me the importance of thinking outside of the box; I learned that sometimes you have to do things that might not feel good, but you do them because they're the right thing to do. Just as much as he'd influenced me, he made sure to be a good man around my boyfriend, too. He made sure he talked to Eric every time he came around, because that was an opportunity to plant those characteristics within him. So that when Eric and I were alone, my dad's lessons would come to mind and defuse a potential argument or something worse. One of the reasons why Eric always said my dad was a pretty cool guy was because that's the impression my dad wanted to leave with him.

So much of the way my father raised us came from what we learn in the Bible. Here are a few of my favorite passages.

Proverbs 22:6: Train up a child in the way he should go and even when he is old he will not depart from it.

Ephesians 6:4: Fathers, do not provoke your children to anger, but bring them up in the discipline and instruction of the Lord.

Proverbs 4:1–2: My children, listen when your father corrects you. Pay attention and learn judgment, for I am giving you good guidance. Don't turn away from my instructions.

1 Corinthians 13:4–7: Love is patient and kind. Love is not jealous or boastful or proud or rude. It does not demand its own way. It is not irritable, and it keeps no record of being wronged. It does not rejoice about injustice, but rejoices whenever the truth wins out. Love never gives up, never loses faith, is always hopeful, and endures through every circumstance.

Fathers, remember that God has equipped you to endure every circumstance you are facing!

My dad wasn't the only man in my life, so it's important that I acknowledge the part my brother Kevin had to play in shaping me as the woman I am today. I am loved by my brother, so the experience of watching his sister struggle through a toxic relationship was hard for him to bear. You can only imagine how that must have felt to not only hear about but also physically see what I went through. He was angry and really had to rely on God in order to control his thoughts and feelings towards Eric. He knew he had to think rationally. My brother and I had a great relationship, but he was newly married and was starting his family, so I didn't want to bother him as much with my problems. He was very protective, and when I wanted some sound advice and prayer, I knew to call him. He didn't want to ruin that, so he rarely asked questions in order to protect our bond.

When Eric came around, he made sure he talked to him but never gave him the third degree like some brothers would have. He was influenced by my dad, so he treated him the exact same way and Eric thought well of him because of that. Like my father, there were some valuable lessons to be learned from my brother and how he treated his sisters.

Here some are points that any man would do well to keep in mind regardless of whether or not they have siblings.

Key Points for Being a Supportive Brother or Sister

- Don't let your anger get in the way. Think of the big picture and be patient.
- Think rationally. This also includes patience, because it reminds you to look before you leap into something you could regret later.
- Your actions have consequences. Your sibling's partner is watching you—and how you interact with them has an effect you may not realize.
- Be involved, and stay involved. Don't get in the way, but let your sister or brother know you're there for them and you care. Even if it seems like no one cares, or they don't need you right now—they will at some point. Be loyal and keep the connections open.

These are points that any man—or woman, for that matter—would do well to keep in mind regardless of whether or not they have siblings. When you allow your anger to get in the way, you cause more harm than good. If you don't think rationally, you'll end up behind bars or worse, while the other person is free; in the end both sides of the aisle suffer from the decisions you made.

Be involved with your sister. Ask her questions about her significant other, even when you don't necessarily agree with her. Make sure that you approach her in a loving way so that she understands you're asking out of concern rather than just being judgmental. My brother has always, and still does, make me feel like he has my back.

Here are a few more Bible verses that support the case for being strong brothers and sisters.

Matthew 5:44: But I say to you, Love your enemies, bless them that curse you, do good to them that hate you, and pray for them which spitefully use you and persecute you.

James 1:19–20: My dear brothers and sisters, take note of this: Everyone should be slow to speak and slow to become angry, because human anger does not produce the righteousness that God desires.

Proverbs 15:18: A hot-tempered person stirs up conflict, but the one who is patient calms a quarrel.

Brothers, remember that God has equipped you to endure every circumstance you are facing!

CHAPTER 8

Know Your Worth

As women, we need to realize our worth. It's important to set standards and to follow them. The best decision I could have ever made was rededicating my life back to Christ. I had praying parents, and through those prayers God blocked a lot of potential hardship. He allowed some things to happen in order to help me become the young lady that I am today. I've caused hurt and pain to enter my family's heart because of the decisions I made. But as we read in Luke 6:28: "Bless those who curse you, pray for those who mistreat you."

Now that I'm out of the toxic situation I stayed in for too long and I can look back at everything, I can understand the decisions I made. In the beginning, I gave someone a chance, not realizing the agony I was putting myself through. Of course, men always want to show you and give you their best, but once they know they can get you to believe they are even a tad bit interested, all hell will break loose. A simple "I love you," "I need you," "You're always there for me" from him every few days is enough for us to keep going back. I was tied to Eric emotionally, mentally, and physically; he was the man I'd lost my virginity to. The Bible reminds us that people will do things on purpose to hurt us, not knowing that they're allowing the enemy to use them.

2 Corinthians 6:14: Do not be unequally yoked together with unbelievers. For what fellowship has righteousness in common? Or what fellowship can light have with darkness?

Coming from a Christian household, I knew this better than most. I still thought I was ready to go off and live my life and do what I wanted to do. When you choose to have sex out of marriage, you're pretty much asking for destruction. I was a believer and I was saved, but Eric wasn't. So, the longer I stayed with him, the dimmer my light became until eventually, I became darkness right along with him.

We ask ourselves why are we so attached when we aren't even in love? A lot of us don't know that it's a spiritual battle with our flesh. This is also known as "Soul Ties." When you choose to have sex, you're giving yourself to your partner, which then makes you vulnerable and connected. This is where sickness and disease come in because you are not only tied to him, but to his previous partners, to their previous partners, and so on.

I knew it wasn't right, but the desires of my flesh took over and changed my way of thinking. The decisions I made were the result of deciding to put God second and a man first. That's why it's so important to wait until marriage, because the Bible talks about man and woman becoming one flesh, bound together so that they can build a healthy relationship with one another.

Matthew 19:5: For this cause shall a man leave father and mother, and to be united [cleave] to his wife, and two will become one flesh.

I had some close friends ask why I didn't do certain things with them. Reflecting on the previous verse from 2 Corinthians, where it says unequally yoked and light having fellowship with darkness, the answer is pretty simple. The Bible talks about repentance and turning away from those sins you were once battling with. Jesus is the light; he is the light that shines through his people. The moment I let go of everything that was not of God, I began to change, and so did my surroundings. You have to be careful who you surround yourself with, especially with those that are in darkness.

When my drinking and partying days were over, I noticed that I didn't have as many people to turn to, but I wasn't upset. I love all my friends, but I love myself first, and I had to do what was best for me and what made me truly happy. At the end of the day, that was Jesus.

So I say to the young mother: You want your family to work, right? In the beginning, the father of your kids was there and it seemed perfect. Or maybe he was never there but because you never had a father in your life, you wanted your child to have what you didn't. Perhaps you don't think you're good enough and have low self-esteem. Maybe his previous girlfriend was beautiful, so you feel as if you need to compete. This list goes on, but I will tell you why there shouldn't even be a list.

One of the reasons why our relationships don't work is because of the foundation that they are set on. If God is truly the number one priority in your life and you are constantly pursuing God, your relationships will never fail. If a man seeks after God and builds a relationship with him, then God will teach him how to really love you. As women, we need to prepare for the man we claim to want.

If *you* aren't right, then you'll never get Mr. Right.

Remember, it is not your job to find your husband; it is his job to find *you*. Some of us struggle with insecurities because of what we're told, or from a previous bad experience. Maybe you were lied to and cheated on. It will take time to heal, and that's fine. But know that things will never get better until you decide to let those old hurts go. Take down those old pictures that are holding you in the painful past—whether they're real pictures, like mine were, or mental images that are replaying in your mind and holding you hostage. And ask God to remove any insecurities you feel so that you can be secure with what God says about you.

Psalm 37:4: Delight yourself in the Lord, and he will give you the desires of your heart.

Proverbs 18:22: He who finds a wife finds a good thing, and obtains favor from the Lord.

Men treat us the way they do because we allow them to; when you have their child, it only gets worse. Does he provide? Is he using you for sex? When you find security within yourself, he'll realize that he's lost you. Men know they can control us because we've given them the power emotionally, physically, sexually, and mentally. He only wants what he knows you'll give him freely. The ups and downs, going through the motions, lying to yourself and saying that you're happy even though you know you're hurting inside isn't healthy. Your children see it just as much as he does, and guess what? He doesn't care. Don't believe what society is feeding us when they say that all men are the same, because it's not true. Some men really do reflect the ideal that God wanted them to be. What sets us all apart is God.

You have to know who you are and be confident in what you believe. If you give a man the satisfaction to letting him walk all over you, he will. (And if you're with a man who would feel satisfaction doing that—head for the door *now*.) Never lower your standards for anyone; if he doesn't like the way you are, then he is not for you.

Yet it's not easy to move on from a long-term relationship, especially when you feel comfortable with it—at least most of the time. Your man might try things from time to time like asking to take you out or seeing how long he can keep you on the phone. When you've allowed things to happen during the relationship, it's going to be hard for him to realize you've moved on and will no longer tolerate his old behavior. He will probably try to win you back, and he might try to blame your decision to leave him on someone else. He might say things like "Who's been in your head?" or "You must be with someone else"—as if you wouldn't make the decision to leave him on your own.

But go ahead and be honest. Tell him you value yourself, and that you deserve to feel good about your life and your relationships. As women, we have to be strong enough to *not* pick up the phone. We have to be strong enough *not* to fall back into our old ways.

Don't allow yourself to be manipulated. If you want to be free, then be strong enough to walk away and don't fall for the various excuses your partner will try to feed you to explain why he isn't treating you right. "I didn't mean it, baby. It won't happen again." Okay, let him use that excuse one time. Give him one second chance. After that, close the door and find someone who really does deserve you, and shows you how much he values you by the way he treats you.

Actions really do speak louder than words.

Of course, the excuses will continue to pour in. Some really might be valid. We all make mistakes. Some of us really did come from lousy backgrounds. I'm not telling you to avoid guys who give you these excuses, but be cautious. Again, they get one second chance, and then it's time to move on.

Here are some excuses you will likely hear:

He was the victim of abuse or grew up in an abusive environment.

A lot of men will try and make excuses for who they are. Maybe he lived in an abusive home when he was young; maybe his father took out his frustrations on the family, or maybe his mother didn't know how to protect her kids. Many women think that because their boyfriend has witnessed some physical abuse, that it's all they know. While I believe that a person's upbringing can have a negative effect on what they dish out in their individual lives, we should always hold ourselves accountable for our own actions. Never let a man get away with being abusive toward you or anyone else, regardless of his background. A real man learns and watches from his surroundings, and he can find a way to move beyond his past. Either he wants to do better or he'll end up being the same man he grew up around.

He's been through a lot, and he's under a lot of stress.

It's possible for real men to release their anger in ways that don't include you. They can hit a punching bag or shoot hoops or join an adult football league. A man who is self-aware will seek counseling for his personal issues, and there are plenty of counselors out there who are willing to help. Sure they might have to pay something, but you get what you pay for—and isn't it worth a few bucks to get your life back on track?

As the woman, you should be your man's confidant, someone he can confide in, who he can go to in more than just the physical sense. Keep his issues confidential, of course; treat him the way you'd want to be treated if you were sharing your innermost thoughts and fears. If money is causing him stress, help him—and yourself—by living frugally and not spending money on stupid stuff that doesn't bring lasting joy.

I deserved it.

You what?! Listen: NO ONE deserves to be hit, smacked around, bullied, intimidated, or humiliated. No one, ever. Not you, not your kids, not your man—no one. Treating others with respect and kindness starts in our own hearts, and goes out into the world from there. Would you let a man hurt your child? Of course not. Then don't let him hurt your child's mother—you!—either.

Never let a man have you thinking you deserve to be smacked around. As women, we are very emotional, and most men—or should I say most immature men—don't understand that about us. Sometimes, we can want a little more attention than usual, but for the most part, we want to be heard and understood. When you allow yourself to think you deserve to be abused, he knows it and will continue to hurt you. Take a stand, embrace your own strength, and don't allow a man to make you feel like you're the bad guy—because you're not. Walk away and let him deal with his own personal issues.

CHAPTER 9

Get Out

The first step to finding yourself is to get out of a toxic relationship—and to do that before it's too late. Whether it's an outright abusive relationship, or you just feel like you're stuck emotionally and mentally, if it's not helping you grow but is instead making you feel miserable or even afraid, then get out. Escaping an unhealthy relationship may seem impossible, but believe me, it isn't.

Here are the steps I took when I finally got to the breaking point and knew it was time to exit the toxic relationship.

1. Ask yourself if you are really done. Have you cried your last tear? I know for myself that I started to feel like I didn't care about the relationship anymore or what he had to say. Nothing he said mattered to me anymore. I just didn't care, because I didn't value him as a part of my life. That's when I knew that we had run our course as a couple.

2. Slowly back off. Stop answering his phone calls and jumping to attention whenever he demands it of you. The less interest I showed in Eric, the more he wanted my attention and the harder he worked to get it. Soon our power dynamics shifted. Once a man knows he has no more power in your relationship, he will try and do anything to get it back. Be prepared for this, but stay strong.

3. Open up and be honest with him, and let him know that you no longer want to continue your relationship the way it's going. This way he knows how you really feel. He may not believe you, in which case he will say things to try and suck you back in: "I promise I'll change," "I love you," "I can't live without you." Or, he might even say negative things to you to try and make you feel bad: "You don't love me," "You were never really there for me," "You got another man," and the list goes on. The goal is to try and make you second-guess yourself, but never put yourself second; remember, you come first!

4. Do things you think are necessary for you to move on. Change your number and block him from social media. Those are things I had to do for me because Eric and I ended on a bad note. While it worked for me, this might not work for you. However, to completely get over someone, I would definitely advise taking the necessary steps so that your feelings won't get caught up and so that you don't have to deal with the extra drama.

5. Surrender and give your life to Christ. If you are already a Christian and you feel that God wouldn't be pleased with the way you've been living, then rededicate your life to him. It was the best decision I ever made, and it helped me move on. Because without God and his love, I wouldn't be here sharing my testimony with you. I tried over and over on my own, and there were days when I thought I was happy and tried hard to make myself believe that I was. But God makes all things new, and he is the only person able to turn it all around and take all the pain away. Only then will you be able to experience what real love is. If you haven't given your life to Christ and you want your life to change, first repent for of all the sins you have committed and ask God to forgive you. Read Romans 10:9 (see below). If you declare with your mouth that Jesus is Lord, and believe in your heart that God raised him from the dead, you will be saved. For it

is with your heart that you believe and are justified, and it is with your mouth that you profess your faith and are saved.

6. Once you've accepted Christ in your life, draw close to him. That means that you must pray, read the Bible, and—if you can—find a church where you feel truly comfortable. Being patient and trusting in God is so important because throughout this time, God is going to teach you how to trust him. The process may not be easy. Being single after being in a relationship for so long will no doubt be difficult, because the thought of being alone can be scary. But no matter how you feel, remember that you're never on your own. Once you get to a place where you understand that God is your friend, he'll always be with you. With him on your side, making the choices that are best for you become easier, and Christ will start to move on your behalf.

Romans 10:9: If you declare with your mouth, "Jesus is Lord," and believe in your heart that God raised him from the dead, you will be saved.

Psalm 139:14: Be strong. Be brave. Be fearless. You are never alone.

Joshua 1:9: She is clothed in strength and dignity, and she laughs without fear of the future.

Proverbs 18:24: One who has unreliable friends soon comes to ruin, but there is a friend who sticks closer than a brother.

Psalm 147:3: He heals the brokenhearted and binds up their wounds.

CHAPTER 10

Heaven

Everyone makes New Year's resolutions, but few people actually follow through with them. I don't believe in empty promises. If you want to change, then make up in your mind that you're going to do so and follow through. My decision to do that just so happened to be at the end of the year, so I took it as a sign. After cutting Eric out of my life, I told myself that I wanted change. I was tired of feeling the way I did—so unhappy and full of hurt, pain, anxiety, and anger. I told God that I was ready, that I needed him to change me and to take all of the junk out of me.

That's exactly what he did. And when New Year's Eve rolled around, I didn't go out and party. Instead, I welcomed the New Year at church, and it was the best decision I ever made for myself.

As time passed, I was speaking with Eric less and less. It was hard for me, and I would always pray and ask God to help me, because after almost four years, I was used to being with someone. I started going back to church with my dad after a two-year hiatus. I was reading my Bible more and praying just to keep me going and focused, because that's all I knew to do. I surrendered my life back to Christ, and he honored that commitment and was able to give me my peace and joy in return.

Around March, my sister Danielle and I were talking about my old friend Taylor, the boy I liked back in middle school and the "Mr. Right" who took me to my junior prom. It was fun remembering back to him. She asked me if I'd talked to him lately and I told her no. I figured it would be a little weird because we hadn't talked in a while, but considering the twelve years of friendship we shared, I figured he'd be happy to hear from me. Or so I hoped. So, one day, I decided to text him to see how he was.

"I was just in the middle of texting you," he replied.

Talk about coincidences!

Taylor was down the street from my house and was going to stop by, but something came up and it didn't happen. I missed our friendship, so we immediately set up a day to meet at Starbucks to talk and catch up.

We met around three in the evening and didn't leave each other's company until that night. It felt like the old days; we just picked up where we'd left off as if no time had passed at all. At first, we worried people would think we were crazy. We were both getting out of serious relationships that had lasted for years, and after three weeks of talking we decided to start dating.

I never paid for a meal, and let me tell you—we ate out a few times a week. I wasn't used to a boyfriend taking care of me, so I really had to train my thoughts: "It's okay, Nay, let him take care of you." His hugs were warm and his kisses were perfect. He made me feel so safe and secure whenever he was in my presence. I often thought to myself, "This is too good to be true," and "When is he going to yell at me or pick a useless fight with me?" I couldn't grasp this is really my true love, the love I've always wanted and admired for years.

Taylor would have "just because" flowers delivered to my house often, and he was the first man outside of my dad to ever give me flowers. I'm not sure why, but receiving those flowers triggered something inside of me and I almost cried. I texted him because he was at work. I wrote: "I love you. You are a dream come true."

He then replied he was glad I liked the flowers, but he didn't say he loved me back. And that's when things took a turn.

We went on a date to an art museum in Sacramento, and he didn't seem himself—he was very disconnected, like he didn't want to be there. Later that night he told me he needed to take some time to himself because he knew he couldn't properly love me and be all I needed him to be, because he was still hurting from his previous relationship. I was crushed and upset, honestly. I didn't want to hear that, because I had been waiting so long for him—to me it almost felt like a heartbreak. Whether I liked it or not, he took his time. He hopped on a plane and went out to visit his family in Chicago for two weeks.

It had reached about a month and although we were still in communication, we still weren't together. I decided to meet up with him and let him know how I felt. Either he was in, or he was out. After we talked, he told me he was ready to fully commit to me and start fresh. We planned to go to the fair as our official first date, and now we go annually as a reminder of where it "really" started.

Some months passed by and I surprised him with a new jersey and tickets to Staples Center to see his favorite basketball player, Kobe Bryant, play. Unfortunately he was there but wasn't playing due to an injury, but we still enjoyed being there. When we arrived back home from Los Angeles, Taylor and I stood in his driveway. He grabbed my hands, looked down at me, and said, "I love you." Of course I grinned—with butterflies shooting everywhere in my stomach—and said, "I love you, too."

Later I realized how important it was for him to take that break from me. God needed to do some work in him so Taylor could be the man He called him to be, not only for me but also for himself. I didn't have to live in fear anymore or worry about him changing throughout our relationship. His heart will always seek after God; therefore, he will always seek and ask God how to love me specifically, and help fulfill my wants, needs, and desires. God will show him how to love, care, nurture, and protect me. That's the beauty of being patient and trusting God through the process.

Let me give you a reason to believe in the power of prayer and the power of praying parents. Taylor and I grew up in the same church, and one day after the service my dad and I saw him and his girlfriend at the time at hotdog stand in the city. God showed my dad that Taylor was stagnant and wouldn't be able to answer the call on his life if he stayed in that relationship, so in that moment my dad prayed a personal prayer for Taylor. This all happened a couple a months before Taylor and I reached out to one another.

I'm sharing this because a simple prayer changed our lives for the better. Since the start of our relationship, my husband acknowledged the call on his life to be a minister of the gospel and has since served as a youth leader. He is now the youth pastor at our church, and I serve beside him as the administrator. He works hard to provide for me and our boys and is an exceptional father. I always say in my eyes he is perfect because he is perfect for me. I thank God for loving me so much to bless me with such an honorable man.

When you know, you know, and I'd known he was the one for me when I was seventeen. Here was my second chance. Believe me, I wasn't going to mess things up again. Finally, it felt like I was living my fairytale with my prince charming.

After dating for about a year and a half, Taylor proposed to me. It felt so unreal. I couldn't believe it, but of course, I said "yes!" We planned our wedding in eight months, and I married the love of my life on July 12, 2015. Married life has been everything I expected. I feel God's love through my husband every day.

I am thankful for what God has done and will do for me in the future, all because I remained faithful to him. These days, my life is peaceful, joyous, and full of love and happiness. I couldn't say that before.

To be in Hell for that season of my life only to find myself in Heaven now is an indescribable feeling. It was worth the wait. Though as I look back, I imagine what I might have told my younger self when she was with Eric: Sweetheart, you don't have to put yourself through this. You don't have to go through Hell before you get to Heaven.

CHAPTER 11

My Supernatural Childbirth

My sister Danielle asked me if I'd ever read the book *Supernatural Childbirth*. I told her no, so she bought it for me. From the moment I started to read it, I couldn't put it down. It blessed me in so many ways that people thought I was crazy when I explained how it had shaped my birth experience.

Let's rewind. Before I read *Supernatural Childbirth*, I'd always told myself I wouldn't be your typical pregnant woman. True to form, I never had morning sickness or even food cravings, and I didn't act ugly toward my husband or make him get food for me in the middle of the night. I was blessed all the way around.

I was amazed by how the author talked about using positive affirmations and prayer for specific outcomes before and during labor. God answered her requests, and I knew that he would bless me as well. I started to claim certain things about my labor and delivery and decided to share them with my husband because I knew he'd agree with me. I also shared my plans with my mom. I told them that I would experience no pain because Jesus had paid for it already. He died on the cross so I wouldn't have to experience pain. I told them that I would only be in labor for three hours, and they said okay.

My mom was taking a healing class at our church and she sent me a photo of an assignment she had. It talked about various things, but what stuck out to me was that it said a woman should be in labor for three hours. I thought, *Wow, God, this is you,* so I continued speaking my truth both aloud and in my head.

At my 20-week anatomy scan, we got confirmation that we were having a baby boy. My cervix showed that I measured at a 2.1, which is considered short. A normal cervix is between 3 to 4 cm. My OB/GYN called me after she spoke with a high-risk doctor (called a perinatologist) about me, who ordered a nightly vaginal dose of progesterone up until I reached 36 weeks. When I saw the perinatologist for the first time that next week, I was 21 weeks and a few days, and he checked my cervix. It was at 3 cm, but when he put pressure on my stomach, it would go back down to 2 cm. As a result, he wanted me to continue taking the progesterone pill every night.

I was a little disappointed because I'd prayed to God for a miracle so that I wouldn't have to take the medication any longer; therefore, hearing that I needed to continue them was disappointing for me. The only positive thing we got from that appointment was that our son was already 1 lb 4 ounces and measured a week ahead of his due date, so we knew he was a strong, healthy, baby already.

When I was 22 weeks pregnant, we saw our doctor again, and he said my cervix had shortened again. I was told that I needed to get steroid shots to help his lungs develop in case he came early, and that I would also need to be put on modified bedrest. In order to work successfully, the steroid shots had to be taken twice in a 24-hour window. I took one that day and went back for the second one 24 hours later. Afterward, I was a little weak because of how overwhelmed I was with everything I was taking—first the progesterone pills and then the steroid shots. That visit didn't sit well with us because my doctor really didn't explain much and rushed through my appointment, so my husband and I decided to switch doctors for future visits.

Our new doctor really seemed to care about me and my baby. He was very thorough and explained that if our son were to come before 37 weeks, it would be our decision whether we wanted to resuscitate him or not. I don't know about you, but just hearing that made me think that my son would live, and from that moment on I kept that belief in front of me. I had to do what was necessary to keep my baby inside of me, so being a couch potato was just something I got used to. Two weeks after that appointment, I started to have strong contractions and immediately went into labor. I had to be monitored for hours while they gave me magnesium to get the contractions to stop. After a while they did, so I was able to go home.

At around 29 weeks, the contractions started up again so I returned to the hospital. It was decided that since Vacaville Kaiser didn't have a NICU (neonatal intensive care unit), I had to be taken to Roseville via ambulance just in case my son came early. I was given another round of steroid shots. (Did I mention that those shots hurt?) Even so, all I could think about was that my son would live. I would do whatever I had to do to ensure as much. The hospital was able to get my contractions under control a second time and sent me on my way.

My husband and I decided we would name our son Nehemiah, after the Old Testament prophet who rebuilt the wall in Jerusalem; his name means "comforted by God." We knew there was no mistake when it came to his name because we definitely needed God's comfort through that whole experience. We prayed together and continued to believe that Nehemiah would come on May 25th. Our doctor had told us that the baby needed to make it to at least 37 weeks to be considered full-term. Nehemiah rebuilt the wall in Jerusalem on the 25th day of the month, and it just so happened that on May 25th I would be 37 weeks pregnant. So, we prayed and believed that God would deliver for us.

On May 13, when I was 35 weeks pregnant, I felt my contractions starting to get strong again. I was sent off for another ambulance ride to a different hospital this time. I had to stay overnight so they could monitor Nehemiah closely. They did a cervical check to see if I was dilated, and I was actually at 3 cm and 70% effaced. I said to myself, *No, God. I prayed for a full-term baby so, he's not coming today.* The next day was Mother's Day, so everyone kept saying that it would be the perfect gift; but I just didn't want it to happen. We—Taylor, Nehemiah, and I—weren't ready yet. Hours later, because I wasn't progressing enough to stay, they sent me home.

At 36 weeks, I was told I could stop taking the progesterone pills. I'd waited so long to stop taking them that the news was a cause of celebration for me. I did a lot of research and reading while I was pregnant since I was on bedrest, and I found out that once you stopped taking the pills, your baby could come within a week—which is exactly what happened.

On May 22, my water broke right when I was about to lie down for bed. I'd thought that once your water broke, that labor would progress fairly quickly, but that wasn't the case for me. At the hospital, the nurses kept asking if I needed any pain medicine, even though they knew my birth plan was to go natural. After 24 hours went by, they decided it was best to induce me to speed things up. I was upset, but I let them do it. The contractions grew stronger but were still nowhere where they needed to be. I walked around, bounced on a ball, and still no baby. The nurse did a cervical check, and I was still 3 cm. That's when I broke down. All I could think about was the *Supernatural Childbirth* book and wondering why I wasn't progressing.

After 30 hours, they offered me a shot to relax my body so that I could get some rest. I knew it was going to make my baby sleepy, and sure enough, it did. By 36 hours, a doctor came in and said that Nehemiah's heart rate wasn't responding to my contractions the way it needed to, so it would be best to get him out by C-section. Actually, even before the doctor walked in to tell me this, I knew what he was going to say. So I was ready, and quickly responded, "Please do what you have to do in order to get Nehemiah here safely."

My husband agreed despite our reservations, and on May 24, 2017, at 11:53 a.m., Nehemiah Taylor was born. The moment I heard his cry, I cried. My sacrifice and his father's sacrifice had not been in vain because we gained a son.

I asked God what I needed to learn from this experience. Why had things gone the opposite of what I'd planned and prayed for? The first couple of months I kept praying and asking God these questions until he finally revealed some things to me.

"Didn't I answer your prayers?" he reminded me, "You asked to get your son here safe; you believed that I would do it, so I did. You did have a supernatural childbirth, even though it wasn't like the ones you read about. Do you remember being in pain? You took no pain medication for 36 hours. You prayed for him to come at 37 weeks, and because you believed in me, I got him here a day before."

What I realized was that my faith got my son into the world safely, even if things didn't really go as planned. Our son got here when God wanted him to enter the world. My faith grew even more from that experience and taught me to rely only on God and not myself.

Hebrews 11:1: Now faith is the substance of things hoped for, the evidence of things not seen.

I'm here to tell you to never give up on yourself. You're beautiful and deserve whatever your heart desires. Let me be an example for you; if he did it for me, he can do it for you.

God bless!

EPILOGUE

What Does Your Heaven Look Like?

I want you to write out what your heaven looks like. What do you want God to do in your life so you can have that healthy relationship He wants you to have?

Write down your thoughts here.

I'd like God to:

1. _____
2. _____
3. _____
4. _____
5. _____

(Grab an extra sheet of paper if you run out of room.)

Now consider what you're willing to sacrifice or let go of in order to let God work his love and miracles in you.

I'm willing to change in this way:

1. _____
2. _____
3. _____
4. _____
5. _____

(Grab another sheet of paper to continue this list.)

Remember to come back to this book and reread your lists. Change them as your circumstances change or as you grow. This should be a lifelong project, actually. When we devote ourselves to God, He guides our paths and leads us into new views of Heaven on Earth.

Mark 11:24–25: I tell you, you can pray for anything, and if you believe that you've received it, it will be yours. But when you are praying, first forgive anyone you are holding a grudge against, so that your Father in heaven will forgive your sins, too.

ACKNOWLEDGMENTS

Mama: Thank you for nurturing me. Thank you for all of your support throughout the years, showing and teaching me how to be a young lady, and how to now be a loving wife and mother. You always have my back when I need you and a lap to cry on.

Daddy: Thank you for being my positive influence, and showing me how a man is supposed to treat his wife and daughters. Your love and support means the world to me, and you are much appreciated.

Nique: My big sister, you taught me how to be strong, and all I had to do was watch you. I appreciate all those prayers and hugs when I needed you; you were right there without me asking. Thank you.

Kevin: Brother, no matter the decisions I made, you never judged me. You just kept on loving me. The love you have for your sisters is indescribable and goes unnoticed. Thank you for praying for and with me with no hesitation; you're the best.

Mela: My twin sister, you were with me the most throughout this journey. I called you about everything, and you always seemed to have the best answer. Thank you for crying tears of pain as well as tears of joy with me.

Nook: My brother from another, I appreciate your love and concern for me throughout the years. You always told me to wipe my tears because things will get better, and you were right; they did.

Danielle: Sister-in-love, you've watched me grow and I will always cherish the bond we share. Thank you for always showing love and support.

Nehemiah: My baby boy, one day you will read this and realize just how special you are to me. You are my miracle baby, and because of you, my faith in God grows stronger each day. Your smile lights up a room, and I love you, my comforter.

Tatum: My second baby boy, you've made me rely on God's strength and not my own. Your first year was difficult for us both, but I would do it over the same way because we persevered through the trials and won. You bring me so much joy and I love you, sweet boy.

Special thanks to my brother-in-love Kevin. Your advice and help was much appreciated—thanks for the support!

I love you all.

Special thanks to Elizabeth Brown of Swift Edits, for sharing your knowledge and helping me bring out my ideas. You are truly gifted!

CPSIA information can be obtained
at www.ICGtesting.com
Printed in the USA
LVHW042304010820
662075LV00005B/425